PMT

PRE MILLENNIUM TENSION

David Lines was born in Nottingham in 1967. Regularly contributing comedy sketches for radio, he also writes for magazines and newspapers and has recently completed his first novel. The author lives in York, and is married to Samantha.

John Abbott was born in Toronto, Canada, before settling in the UK where he has made a career in advertising. He currently works for a large agency in N. Yorkshire. As a self confessed game addict, John cites Shigeru Miyamoto as a source of inspiration.

DAVID LINES

Dear Sir or Madam will you read my book?
It took me years to write, will you take a look?
Based on a novel by a man named Lear,
And I need a job so I want to be a paperback writer.

Paperback Writer by John Lennon and Paul McCartney

JOHN ABBOTT

Thanks to my closest friends (you know who you are) for their continuing friendship. Mum, Dad and Bev for their support, everyone at work and all those who E-mailed me. Extra special thanks to Nathan Beer (wall kicks will work) for all his ideas. A big 'Hello' goes out to Samuel, my nephew, and of course my girlfriend Susan for being lovely and wonderful.

E-mail: jon@alien23.demon.co.uk

'He had the skeletal remains of a vole hanging from his mouth and tiny bubbles issued from his nostrils…'

PMT

PRE MILLENNIUM TENSION

David Lines
John Abbott

ARROW

Published in the United Kingdom in 1997 by
Arrow Books

2 4 6 8 10 9 7 5 3 1

First published in the United Kingdom in 1997 by Arrow

Arrow Books Limited
Random House UK Ltd, 20 Vauxhall Bridge Road, London SW1V 2SA

Random House Australia (Pty) Limited
20 Alfred Street, Milsons Point, Sydney, New South Wales 2061, Australia

Random House New Zealand Limited
18 Poland Road, Glenfield, Auckland 10, New Zealand

Random House South Africa (Pty) Limited
Endulini, 5A Jubilee Road, Parktown 2193, South Africa

Random House UK Limited Reg. No. 954009

A CIP catalogue record for this book is available from the British Library

Printed and bound in Belgium

ISBN 0 09 925678 9

Monitoring signals from inter-stellar neighbours appeared less difficult than originally anticipated.

Another spoon-bending disaster...

"Alright my love, do you want to stick with your base card, or try for the Page of Cups?"

Once the cockroaches found out that science had proved they were the only creatures capable of surviving a nuclear holocaust, they soon learned to put up with the odd upset...

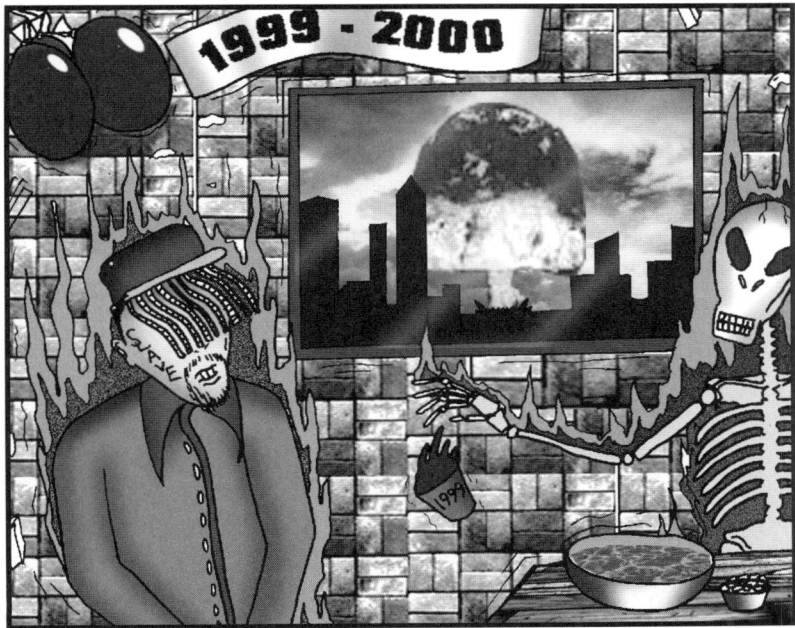

Prince's party didn't quite go off with
the bang he expected.

The publicity department for RTR Records began to regret their new marketing strategy when the Space Girls' audience began to disappear.

A New Age of Modernism.

This year, Mr Geller approached the task of halting Big Ben with refreshing ingenuity.

Upon turning thirty, Ralph finally faced up to the fact that he was 'going grey'.

Miles was amazed at how realistic 'Space Fighter IV' was.

"...it's the subtle differences. You know what they call a Zefal Burger™ with cheese on earth? - they call it a Big-Mac"

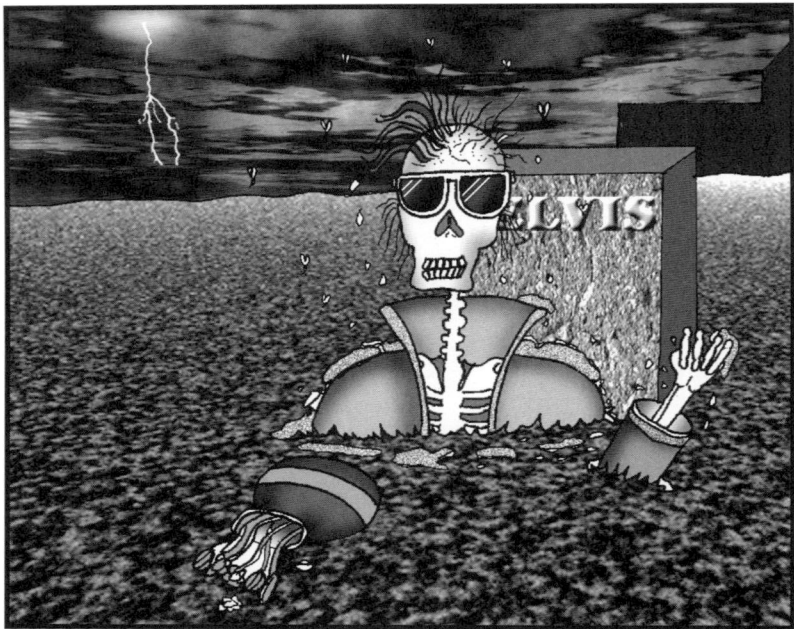

...and thus it was written that The King would rise again to rule over us all.

"It's an open and shut case -
we're looking for a serial homeopath."

As the millennium approached, reports of animal rainfall became more bizarre.

After the Apocalypse, some of the Four Horsemen tried selling donkey rides on Blackpool beach.

In the late 1990's, inducing ectoplasm
was a little more straightforward.

"OK, Arthur - so you give us mobile phones, satellites and then you predict life on Europa. Just where the hell __are__ you from?"

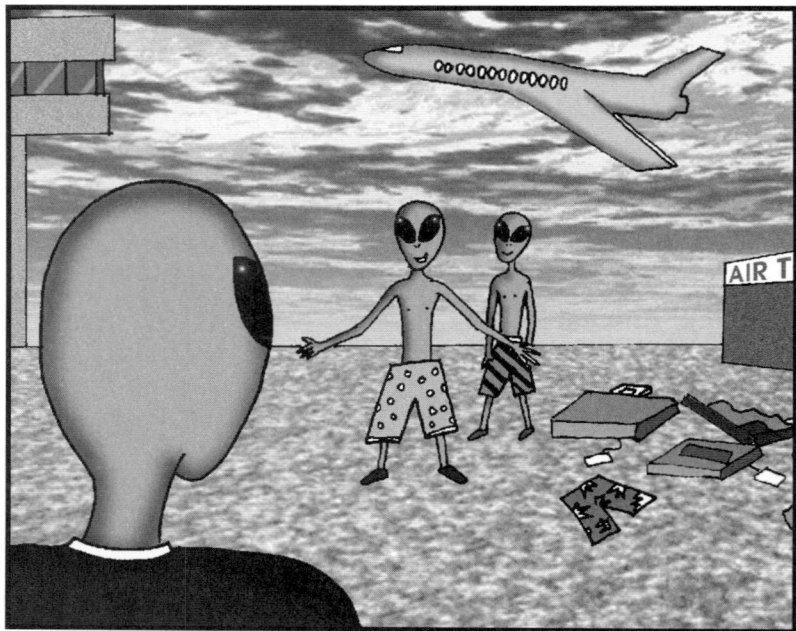

"How many times? It's Planes from Bermuda, not bermudas from planes!"

"Come on Jimmy, it's a little bit late to be playing Twister with Jane."

"Attention all inmates. Welcome to Windscale's Retreat for the Radioactively Affected. Before this evening's millennium celebrations get fully underway, we should like to draw your attention to our strict 'NO Auld Lang Syne' policy ruling. For obvious reasons."

Of course, not everyone was too upset when The Great Floods came.

The anthropologist's discovery of 'Big Foot' proved to be a little disappointing.

Cyber With Rosie

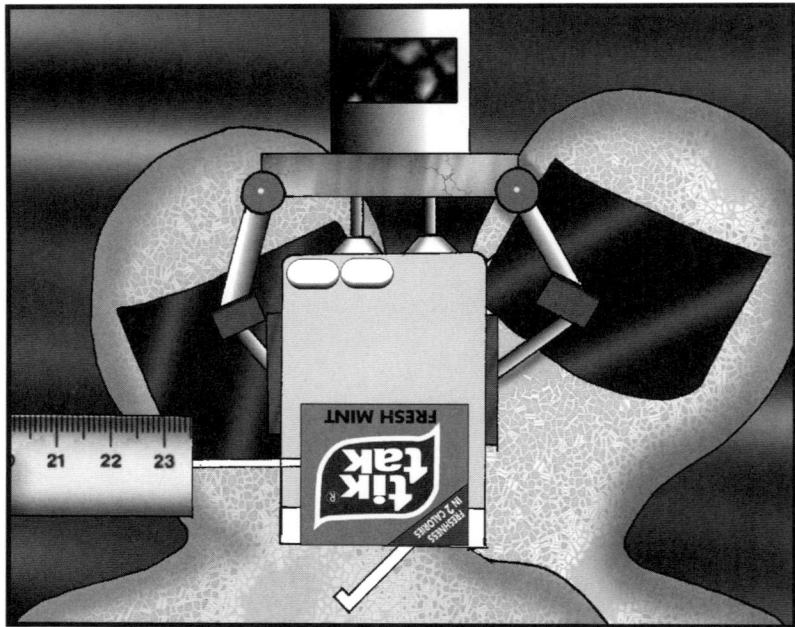

By the millennium, mankind had mastered cold fusion but still could not get to grips with the mysterious forces that bound together the remaining two tik-taks at the bottom of the box.

Swampy's commitment to By Pass Protesting was bordering on the obsessional.

Due to a millennium computer glitch, Agent Bond's code name became '1000775757 Syntax Error'

The Picture of Dorian Grey

So the devil waits 2000 years to bring the apocalypse to The Uplanders. Thankfully, he hadn't banked on technology being so advanced.

"Let me through - I'm a homeopath."

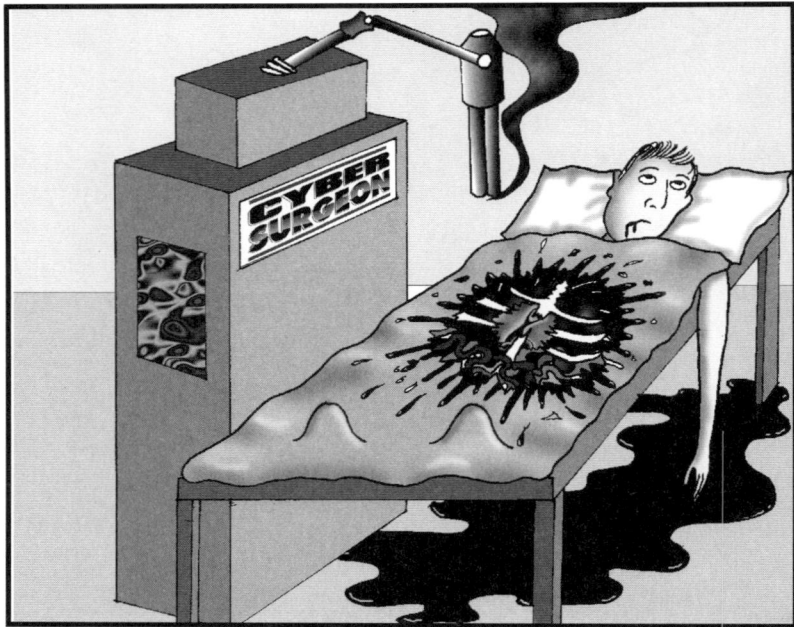

We don't know who programmed the Cybersurgeon, but maybe they should have started by wiping 'Doom' off the network.

"Lucy, Trevor? Stand up, why don't you? Listen, folks - I want you to give a big hand to some friends of mine who flew in tonight all the way from the Belt of Orion..."

Father Jack had learned to deal with Sister Pat's time of the month problems.

Little did the Third Horseman realise just how much his new job was going to take off.

"Don't shoot until you see the blacks of their eyes!"

"Bollocks - in my day it was A Place for Everything
and Everything in its Place."

The first inter-racial screen kiss didn't go down too well.

Researchers agreed that this was indeed a pretty bizarre case of spontaneous combustion.

"Of course we were upset at first, but at least he keeps the lawn looking nice"

(21st Century Music Hall gag)

The Jones' Sunday Dinner was never the same after the nuclear holocaust.

There was no denying it - conclusive evidence that people really do imitate what they see on the television.

"No, you idiot! I said 'Clone the sheep'..."

The comic's editor didn't relish the idea of a name change.

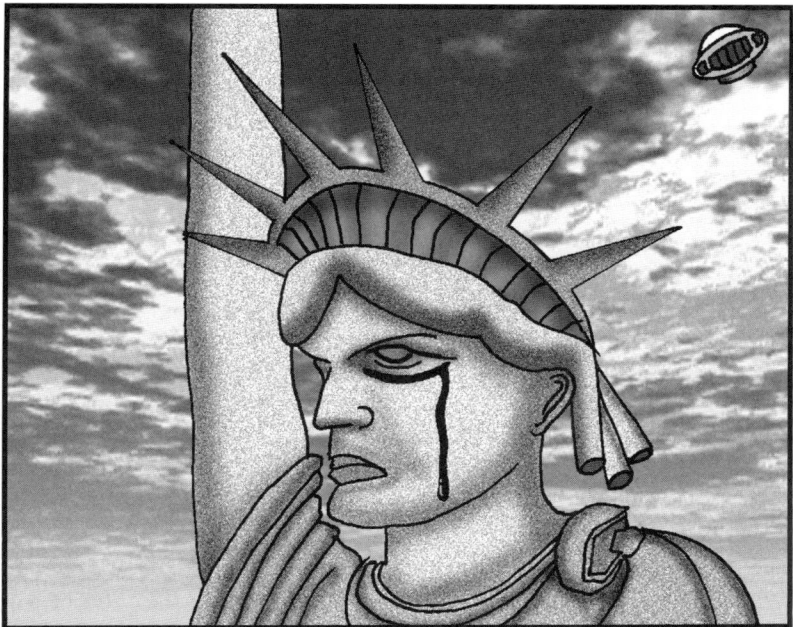

Weeping statues?
Man, you ain't seen nothing yet...

"OK Mary, take a good long look. Try to remember which seamonster burst out of the loch and attacked you. Take your time..."

Suddenly, Roseanne's New Year's calorie counting resolution seemed pretty pointless.

The Beneton ad agency was first on the scene.

People in Biospheres shouldn't throw rock samples.

The thought of seeing in the new year again with
Clive James was bad enough, but The Millennium...

Working on his slice, our friend opted for a 666 iron.

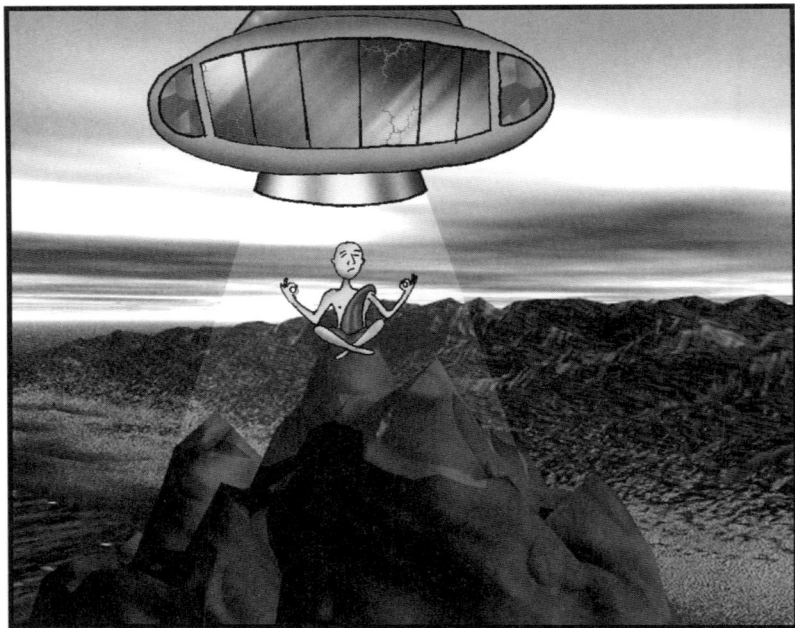

After a hard day's abuducting, the boys liked to stop off for a chinese.

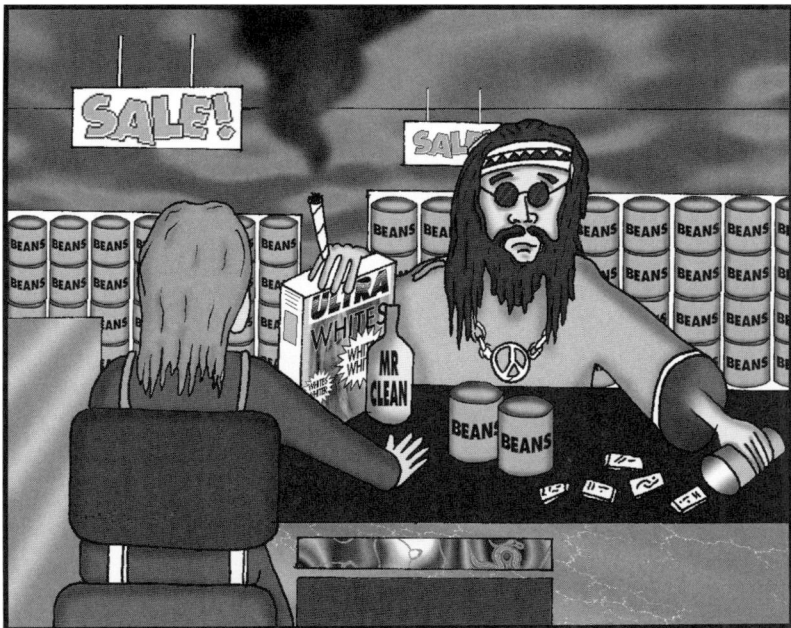

Buy a big box powder or new Super Concentrated?
Maybe the runes can help...

The mysterious slaying of farm animals that many had put down to The Chupacabra had now reached super 'sonic' proportions.

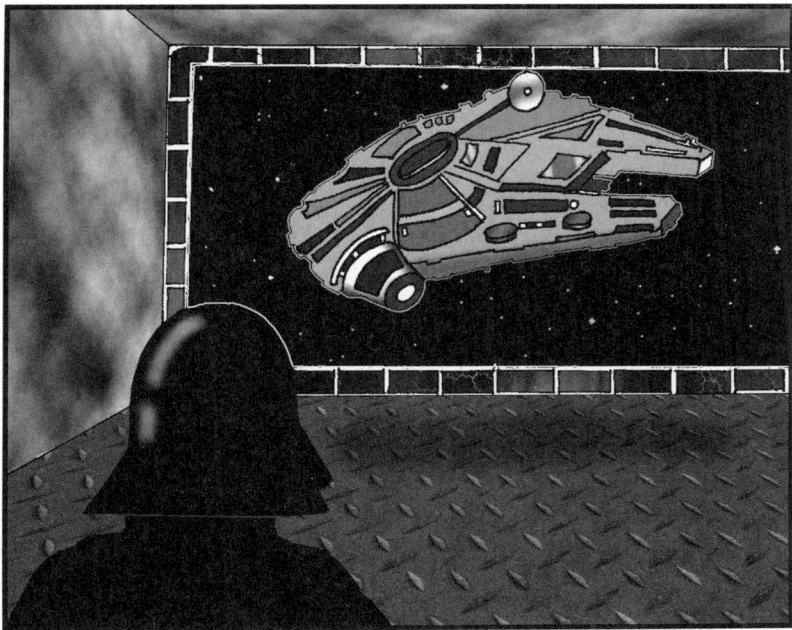

Not everyone was over the moon when it came to seeing in the new millennium.

It was a little too late before Mr. Perkins realised just how much he'd been neglecting his wife...

It was a strange morning for Reginald. His alarm clock told him to wake up, his car told him it needed petrol and his morning grapefruit seeds told him to kill women.

Having discovered Jake's peanut allergy, his schoolfriends took great delight in playing Russian roulette with a bag of Revels.

Firework displays always brought the family together.

The author had developed a cult following. The problem was that the cult who were following him were the Moonies.